Discovering Literature Series

A Teaching Guide to

Roll of Thunder, Hear My Cry

by Jeanette Machoian

Illustration by Kathy Kifer and Marina Krasnik

Roll of Thunder, Hear My Cry

Puffin Books
Published by the Penguin Group
Penguin Books USA Inc.,
375 Hudson Street
New York, New York 10014, USA

Published by:
Garlic Press
605 Powers St.
Eugene, OR 97402

ISBN 0-931993-94-6
Order Number GP-094
Printed in China

www.garlicpress.com

Table of Contents

NOTES TO THE TEACHER

The Discovering Literature Series is designed to develop a student's appreciation for good literature and to improve reading comprehension. While many skills reinforce a student's ability to comprehend what he or she reads (sequencing, cause and effect, finding details, using context clues), two skills are vital: discerning **main ideas** and **summarizing** text. Students who can master these two essential skills develop into sophisticated readers.

The following discussion details the various elements that constitute this Series.

About Chapter Organization

Each chapter analysis is organized into three basic elements: **Student Directives**, **Chapter Vocabulary**, and **Chapter Summary**. Student Directives and Chapter Vocabulary need to be displayed on the board or on an overhead projector after each chapter is read. Students copy the Chapter Vocabulary and write their own summaries following the Student Directives.

The **Student Directives** contain the main ideas in each chapter. They provide the students, working individually or in groups, with a framework for developing their summaries. Student Directives can also be used as group discussion topics.

The **Chapter Vocabulary** includes definitions of key words from each chapter. To save time, students need only to copy, not look up, definitions. Suggestions for teaching vocabulary to students are as follows:

1. Make and display flashcards with the words and definitions. Refer to vocabulary cards in daily review.
2. Have students write sentences individually, in groups, or as a class using the words in the story's context.
3. Give frequent quizzes before an actual test.
4. Have students make their own vocabulary crossword puzzles or word search puzzles.
5. Play 20 questions with vocabulary words.
6. Host a vocabulary bee where the students give definitions for the word rather than spelling it.

A **Chapter Summary** for each chapter is included for teacher use and knowledge. Some students may initially need to copy the summaries in order to feel comfortable writing their own subsequent ones. Other students can use the completed summaries as a comparison to guide their own work. Summary writing provides an opportunity to polish student composition skills, in addition to reading skills.

The **blackline master**, *Chapter Summary & Vocabulary,* is provided on page 57. It can be duplicated for student use. Teachers can also use it to make transparencies for displaying Student Directives and Chapter Vocabulary.

In addition, teachers may opt to have students make folders to house their Chapter Summary & Vocabulary sheets. A sample cover sheet (see page 58) for student embellishments has been provided. Cover sheets can be laminated, if desired, and affixed to a manila (or other) folder.

Sample:
Blackline Master

CHAPTER SUMMARY & VOCABULARY — Roll of Thunder, Hear My Cry

Chapter Title _____ Chapter 2 _____ Name _____

Chapter Summary: **Student Directives**

1. Tell why Papa comes home unexpectedly.
2. Describe Mr. Morrison.
3. Discuss Cassie's suspicion that Mr. Morrison has come to their home to do more than work.
4. Review the trouble in the community.
5. Relate Mr. Logan's warning to his kids about the Wallace store.

Chapter Vocabulary:

1. **scoff**
   to show disrespect; to make fun of

2. **fibrous**
   made of or containing long, slender threads

3. **gait**
   way of walking or running

4. **formidable**
   causing fear, dread, or difficulty

5. **penetrating**
   entering into, going through, or piercing
   (continued on backside)

Sample Transparency:
Student Directives and Chapter Vocabulary

CHAPTER SUMMARY & VOCABULARY — Roll of Thunder, Hear My Cry

Chapter Title _____ Chapter 2 _____ Name _____

Chapter Summary: The Logan children, Mrs. Logan, and Big Ma are picking cotton on Saturday. As they finish for the day, Cassie sees Mr. Logan coming up the road with another man. Papa has brought Mr. Morrison, a quiet giant of a man, to work on their farm because Mr. Morrison lost his job on the railroad. Cassie, however, wonders if Mr. Morrison, who has a massive body bulging with muscles, isn't here to do more than work -- especially, in light of the burnings at the Berry's house. After church the next morning, the Averys and Laniers stop by the Logan house. They expresss their anger and hopelessness for the death of Mr. Berry who has left a wife and six children. Mr. Logan announces to the guests that the Logan family does not shop at the Wallace store, to which he gets no reply. After the guests leave, Papa warns the children sternly that the Wallace store is off limits because it'll bring a whole lot of trouble one day to those kids who go up there after school to buy cigarettes and bootleg liquor.

Chapter Vocabulary:

1. **scoff**
   to show disrespect; to make fun of

2. **fibrous**
   made of or containing long, slender threads

3. **gait**
   way of walking or running

4. **formidable**
   causing fear, dread, or difficulty

5. **penetrating**
   entering into, going through, or piercing
   (continued on backside)

Sample Transparency:
Chapter Summary and Chapter Vocabulary

The above two samples serve to illustrate how the **blackline master**, *Chapter Summary & Vocabulary,* can be used as a transparency to focus student work. These transparencies are particularly effective for displaying Student Directives and Chapter Vocabulary. They are also effective for initially modeling how Chapter Summaries can be written.

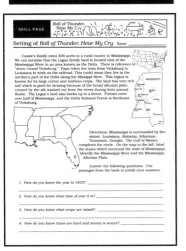

Sample: Skill Page

Skill Pages throughout the series have been developed to increase students' understanding of various literary elements and to reinforce vital reading skills. Since the entire series is devoted to reinforcing **main ideas** and **summarizing** skills, no further work has been provided on these skills. Depending upon each novel, Skill Pages reinforce various skills from among the following: **outlining**; **cause and effect**; **sequencing**; **character, setting, and plot development**; and **figurative language**. You will note that character development is based upon a values framework.

About the
Tests

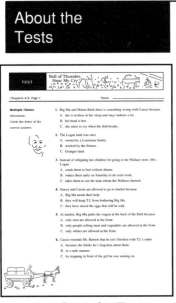

Sample: Test

At the end of each three-chapter block, a comprehensive open-book **Test** has been developed for your use. Each test includes reading comprehension, vocabulary, and short essays.

An Answer Key is provided at the back of the book for each Test.

The vocabulary portion of the Tests may be particularly difficult. You will probably want to give one or two vocabulary quizzes before administering each of the four Tests.

About the
Writer's Forum

Suggestions for writing are presented under the **Writer's Forum** throughout this guide. You can choose from these suggestions or substitute your own creative-writing ideas.

Student Directives

1. Describe the Logan family members and relate their way of life.
2. Relate the treatment the Logan and Avery children receive by the bus driver.
3. Tell what bad news T.J. shares with the Logan children, and introduce Jeremy.
4. Discuss why Little Man refuses his text book and why he is offended.
5. Relate how Mama resolved the problem of the offensive books.

Vocabulary

admonish	to warn or scold gently
raucous	behaving noisily; harsh and unpleasant
pensive	thinking seriously; expressing sad thoughts
undaunted	not discouraged nor frightened
transposed	having changed the order of
penchant	a strong liking for something; ability
temerity	acting without caution; reckless boldness
imperious	arrogant; overbearing; domineering

Summary

Roll of Thunder, Hear My Cry, is told by Cassie Logan, a nine-year old black child in Mississippi in the 1930's. She and her brothers are on their way to their first day of school at Great Faith School. It's October and the white children have been in school since August. Cassie's older brother, Stacey, is twelve, and is going to be in their mother's class. Christopher-John, seven, is a cheerful boy who likes to get along with everyone. Little Man, six, is starting school for the first time, and is trying hard to stay very clean. The Logans own 400 acres of land, half of which is paid for. Mr. Logan works on the railroad in Louisiana most of the year to make enough money to pay the mortgage and taxes. Mr. Logan's mother, Big Ma, takes care of the home. And, all the Logans pitch in to raise cotton, as well. On their walk to school, the children are joined by the Avery brothers: T.J. and Claude. Talkative T.J. tells about Mr. Berry and

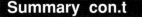

Summary con.t his nephews who were burned by whites the night before. When the white kids' school bus comes by, the driver deliberately sprays them all with dust as the white kids laugh. Jeremy is one white kid, however, who never takes the school bus -- prefering the company of the Logans. Once at school, Little Man is issued a ragged and dirty book. Sure there has been some mistake, he returns it to his teacher for a new clean one. Miss Crocker says he'll keep the one given or have none at all. But, when Little Man notices the chart in the front of the book which indicates that it is too old and worn for the white kids and has been designated for "nigra" children, he stomps on his book. Cassie also refuses the book issued to her. Later, Miss Crocker reports the incident to Mrs. Logan, who makes it clear that she will not punish the children further. Moreover, she affixes a clean page over the offensive chart in each book including those books for her seventh-graders.

About the Characters

Name _____

Directions: Below is a Character Chart to help you organize the characters from the novel. Fill in whatever information is missing—either the character's name or a character description.

Cassie	Little Man	Big Ma
Stacey	Mr. Logan	Jeremy
Mrs. Logan	T.J.	Christopher-John

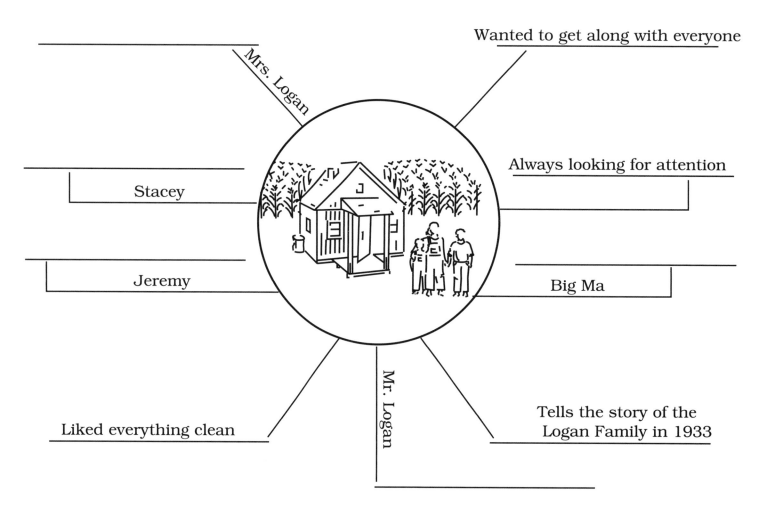

Mrs. Logan

Wanted to get along with everyone

Stacey

Always looking for attention

Jeremy

Big Ma

Liked everything clean

Mr. Logan

Tells the story of the
Logan Family in 1933

Student Directives

1. Tell why Papa comes home unexpectedly.
2. Describe Mr. Morrison.
3. Discuss Cassie's suspicion that Mr. Morrison has come to their home to do more than work.
4. Review the trouble in the community.
5. Relate Mr. Logan's warning to his kids about the Wallace store.

Vocabulary

scoff	to show disrespect; to make fun of
fibrous	made of or containing long, slender threads
gait	way of walking or running
formidable	causing fear, dread, or difficulty
penetrating	entering into, going through, or piercing
glared	stared at angrily
lynched	hanged to death by a mob, usually with no trial

Summary

The Logan children, Mrs. Logan, and Big Ma are picking cotton on Saturday. As they finish for the day, Cassie sees Mr. Logan coming up the road with another man. Papa has brought Mr. Morrison, a quiet giant of a man, to work on their farm because Mr. Morrison lost his job on the railroad. Cassie, however, wonders if Mr. Morrison, who has a massive body bulging with muscles, isn't here to do more than work -- especially, in light of the burnings at the Berry's house. After church the next morning, the Averys and Laniers stop by the Logan house. They expresss their anger and hopelessness for the death of Mr. Berry who has left a wife and six children. Mr. Logan announces to the guests that the Logan family does not shop at the Wallace store, to which he gets no reply. After the guests leave, Papa warns the children sternly that the Wallace store is off limits because it'll bring a whole lot of trouble one day to those kids who go up there after school to buy cigarettes and bootleg liquor.

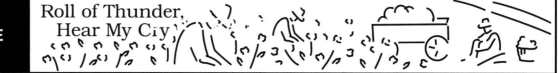

Setting of *Roll of Thunder, Hear My Cry*   Name _____

Cassie's family owns 400 acres in a rural county in Mississippi. We can surmise that the Logan family land is located east of the Mississippi River in an area known as the Delta. There is reference to "down 'round Vicksburg." Papa takes the train from Vicksburg to Louisiana to work on the railroad. This could mean they live in the northern part of the Delta along the Missssppi River. This region is known for its large cotton and soybean crops. The land has very rich soil which is good for farming because of the broad alluvian plain created by the silt washed out from the rivers during their annual floods. The Logan's land also backs up to a forest. Forests cover over half of Mississippi, and the Delta National Forest is Northeast of Vicksburg.

Directions: Mississippi is surrounded by five states: Louisiana, Alabama, Arkansas, Tennessee, Georgia. The Gulf of Mexico completes the circle. On the map to the left, label the states which surround the state of Mississippi. Identify the Mississippi River and the Mississippi Alluvian Plain.

Answer the following questions. Cite passages from the book to justify your answers.

1. How do you know the year is 1933? _____

_____

2. How do you know what time of year it is? _____

_____

3. How do you know what crops are raised? _____

_____

4. How do you know times are hard and money is scarce? _____

_____

Student Directives

1. Discuss why the Logan children are upset about walking to and from school in the rainy weather.
2. Relate how the Logan kids get back at the bus driver.
3. Tell about the news that Mr. Avery brings that night.
4. Review what Cassie sees when she crawls out onto the porch in the night.
5. Describe Cassie's feelings at this point in the story.

Vocabulary

resiliency	springing back; recovering strength quickly
donned	put on
embittered	made bitter or resentful
coddling	pampering; treating tenderly
relent	to give in to pity; to become less harsh
precariously	dangerously; lacking security
cloaking	hiding or covering

Summary

It is now late October and the rains have begun. Besides trying to keep dry on the way to and from school, the Logans daily deal with the school bus from Jefferson Davis School. The driver speeds past, spraying the walking kids with muddy water. They try to watch for the bus in order to climb up the bank of the forest before the bus reaches them, but are not always successful. One morning after a particularly heavy storm when the bus once again makes a mess of their clothing, Stacey devises a plan. During lunch hour, the Logan children dig out a portion of the road and fill it with water. When the bus comes by that afternoon, it stalls in the huge ditch, made even bigger by more rain. The bus is made useless for weeks. That night when Mrs. Logan tells Big Ma about it, not knowing her children's part in it, they all have a laugh over it. When Mr. Avery comes by with a warning that the night men are riding again, Mama sends the children to bed. Though the children, who have huddled together in the boys' room, cannot hear Mr. Avery clearly because of the storm, they are sure the night men know about their part in the intentional crippling of the bus. Later in the night, Cassie is awakened by a noise on the porch. She sneaks outside in time to see seven sets of headlights coming toward their house. The leader of the caravan decides they have the wrong house and the cars retreat. Cassie is trembling as she carefully gets back into bed, unable to sleep until dawn.

Figurative Language: Similes

Name _____

Authors often use figurative language to make their writing more meaningful to the reader. One type of figurative language is the simile. A simile compares two things by using a word such as "like" or "as." The comparison makes the writing more interesting and helps the reader to understand the author's meaning better. An example is:

"He is hungry as a bear."

"He" is being compared to a bear. The comparison (the way they are alike) is that both are very hungry.

Throughout *Roll of Thunder, Hear My Cry*, the author, Mildred D. Taylor, uses similes. These similes serve to make her meaning interesting and clear. An example is when Mrs. Logan says of her children "...they're quiet as church mice." The Logan kids are being compared to church mice. The meaning is that both mice that live in a church and the Logans are being very quiet.

Direction 1: After each simile, list the two things which are being compared and what the comparison is (how they are alike).

---

1. "...allowing it [dust] to sift back onto my socks and shoes like gritty red snow." p.5

2. "...sun-splotched road wound like a lazy red serpent..." p.6

3. "...bus bore down on him spewing clouds of red dust like a huge yellow dragon breathing fire." p.13

4. "She [Miss Crocker] stood up, gazing down upon Little Man like a bony giant..." p. 23

5. "...he [Little Man] sucked in his breath and sprang from his chair like a wounded animal..." p. 24

6. "...the rain fell like hail upon our bent heads." p. 46

7. "a caravan of headlights appeared...coming fast along the rain-soaked road like cat eyes in the night." p.67

8. "Mr. Morrison...moving silently, like a jungle cat, from the side of the house..." p.68.

Direction 2: Find at least two more similes in the first two chapters and continue to identify similes in each new chapter.

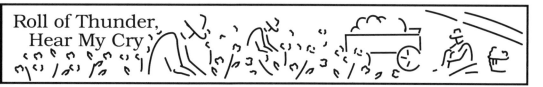
What Do You Think...About Discrimination?

To discriminate means to hold a position or attitude for or against someone based upon unfair reasons, usually by how one appears outwardly (a person's heritage, clothes, wealth, skin color, etc.) For example, African Americans, women, Native Americans, Irish Americans, Japanese Americans have all been denied basic civil and human rights at one time or another based on discrimination.

Consider the following questions.

1. Have you ever gone into a store where the clerk ignores you because there are adults waiting too, even if you were there first?

2. Have you ever heard of an older person being passed over for a job just because a younger person has applied, too?

3. Have you ever found yourself trusting someone who was well-dressed or had a nice car just because of those material things?

4. Have you or someone you know ever thought that a person with a physical disability (in a wheel chair, blind or deaf) was less intelligent than others.

These are all cases of discrimination and this discrimination is a major theme of *Roll of Thunder, Hear My Cry*.

In *Roll of Thunder, Hear My Cry*, the black community is discriminated against in a number of ways. For instance, the county did not provide a school bus or good books for its black students. Also, some blacks were unfairly accused and punished for things they didn't do, as in the Berrys' case.

Direction: Write about an experience you may have had with discrimination.

1. If you discriminated against another person: What happened? Did you realize you were judging unfairly? What did you do? How do you feel about it now?

2. If you were discriminated against: What happened? What did you do? Have you seen the person/people since? How do you feel about it now?

3. Using your experience and the situations in *Roll of Thunder, Hear My Cry* as reference, explain why you think people discriminate against others. What can each of us do to keep this from happening?

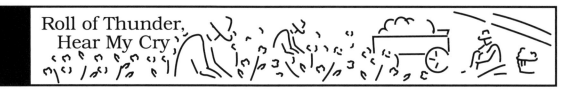
Multiple Choice

Directions:

Circle the letter of the

correct answer.

1. Great Faith School started in October and not in August because

    A. the students at Great Faith were all older so they had been attending school longer.

    B. many of the students who attended Great Faith were needed at home to pick cotton.

    C. Great Faith's school year ended in July and not in May.

2. Little Man wants to keep his clothes clean on the way to school because

    A. he likes everything clean.

    B. he wants to impress his teacher.

    C. Mama warned him to stay clean.

3. Since Stacey and T.J. are going to be in Mrs. Logan's class, T.J. suggests to Stacey that

    A. they study together after school.

    B. they do their class project together.

    C. Stacey try to get answers to tests.

4. Mama fixes the books of her whole seventh grade class, as well as Little Man's and Cassie's,

    A. so the students wouldn't know how old the books were.

    B. because she wanted the students to have a blank page to use for notes.

    C. to eliminate the reminder that the books were the white students' discards.

5. Papa comes home

    A. because Mama wrote and asked him to come.

    B. to bring Mr. Morrison.

    C. because he forgot some papers at home.

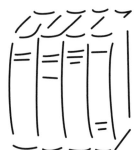

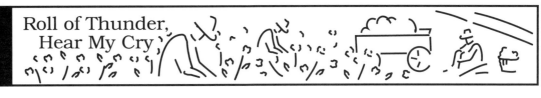
Multiple Choice

Directions:

Circle the letter of the

correct answer.

6. Even though it was not spoken of, it was well known to both blacks and whites that

    A. Jefferson Davis was not as good a school as Great Faith.

    B. Harlan Granger tried to help the blacks.

    C. The Wallaces burned the Berrys.

7. Most of the money for Great Faith School comes from

    A. the churches.

    B. the county.

    C. the students' families.

8. When the Jefferson Davis bus causes the Logan and Avery children to fall into the gully, Stacey promises Little Man that it won't happen again because

    A. Stacey's going to have a talk with Mr. Grimes, the bus driver.

    B. Stacey has a plan to cripple the Jefferson Davis bus.

    C. Stacey knows a different route to school.

9. When Mama tells Big Ma about the Jefferson Davis bus,

    A. the Logan children feel ashamed.

    B. Mama says she's glad it happened.

    C. Big Ma feels sorry for the kids who ride the bus.

10. When Mr. Avery comes to the Logan home late one night and tells Mrs. Logan that the night riders are out again,

    A. Cassie and her brothers are allowed to stay and hear the news.

    B. Big Ma leaves to give another family the news.

    C. Cassie and the boys think the riders are looking for them.

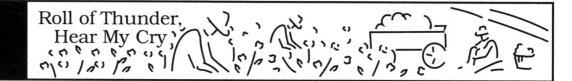
Name _____

Vocabulary

Directions:

Fill in the blank with the correct word.

admonish   penetrating   precariously

penchant   fibrous   relent

temerity   resiliency   scoff

undaunted

1. _____ reckless boldness; acting without caution

2. _____ entering into, going through, or piercing

3. _____ dangerously; lacking security

4. _____ springing back; recovering strength quickly

5. _____ to warn or scold gently

6. _____ not discouraged or frightened

7. _____ to show disrespect

8. _____ strong liking for something; ability

9. _____ to give in to pity; to become less harsh

10. _____ made of or containing long, slender threads

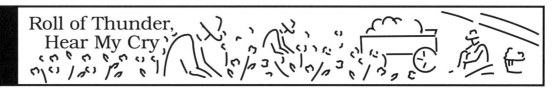
Essay Questions

Directions:

Answer in complete

sentences.

1. Cassie and Little Man are offended by the "throwaway" books the county gives the black students, but Miss Crocker is not. Give examples from the story that show how the Logans' attitude about inequality is different than even some of the other black families. What are some of the things that Mr. and Mrs. Logan do, say, and teach the children that show their ideas?

_____

_____

_____

_____

_____

_____

_____

2. Jeremy is the one white student who never rides their bus. Instead, he meets and walks part way with the Logans. The morning they are forced into the gully by the bus, the Logans refuse to talk to Jeremy. Cassie observes that Jeremy "looked as if the world itself was slung around his neck." Why does he look like this? What makes Jeremy different? From what you have learned about him so far, explain why Jeremy is caught between the two groups, blacks and whites.

_____

_____

_____

_____

_____

_____

_____

Student Directives

1. Describe the Logan children's mood on this Saturday.
2. Discuss Stacey's reluctance to accept Mr. Morrison's presence at the Logan home.
3. Tell about T.J.'s plans to pass Mrs. Logan's test and the resulting fight with Stacey.
4. Relate Mr. Morrison's advice to Stacey.
5. Tell how Mama "punishes" the children, and what she does to stop using the Wallace store.

Vocabulary

pact	agreement
listless	lacking energy or the interest to move
expound	to explain or interpret
prevail	to become common or widespread
feign	to pretend
emphatic	showing or spoken with forceful expression
vex	to bring trouble or worry to; to annoy
patronize	to be a customer of

Summary

This Saturday, Mama and Big Ma comment on how Cassie and her brothers are listless and quiet. They wonder if the kids saw the night riders, but decide against that horrible thought. T.J. shows up with the tale that the night riders tarred and feathered Mr. Tatum, worrying the Logan kids more. Awhile later, Stacey catches T.J. at Mrs. Logan's desk, suspecting he is trying to get test answers. Cassie gets Stacey to reveal his resentment towards Mr. Morrison. Stacey thinks he is fully capable of taking care of the family while Papa's away. On the way to school the following Monday, T.J. reveals his cheat notes for the test. Stacy rips them up but T.J. makes another set. To avoid getting caught, he slips the notes onto Stacey's desk. Subsequently, Stacey is whipped in front of the class. After school, T.J. runs down to Wallace's store, thinking Stacey will never follow him there. But, Stacey does follow and the rest of the Logan kids, too. Mr. Morrison fortunately was there with the wagon. The fight broke up and Mr. Morrison took the worried children home. Mr. Morrison told Stacey that he'd not tell about the fight. Understanding this silent advice, Stacey decides to confess to Mama about going to the Wallace store. The children are amazed that there has been no punishment other than a scolding. But, the real punishment comes the following Saturday when Mama takes them to Mr. and Mrs. Berry and they observe firsthand the Wallaces true cruelty. On their return, Mrs. Logan stops to talk to families she knows, and encourages them not to shop at the Wallaces.

Understanding Direction

Name _____

Direction is a big part of the Setting in a story. A good storyteller can bring the reader into the characters' homes, schools, or other environment. For instance:

> The living area of the Logan home is also Mama and Papa's room. From this room, Cassie and Big Ma's room can be reached as well as the kitchen, the boys' room, and both the front and one side porch (page 35). Cassie and Big Ma's room opens onto the front porch (page 61) and the boys' room onto one side porch. We know that Mr. Morrison lives in the tenant shack in the south pasture (page 77), which is within yelling distance of the back porch (page 78). Although it's hard to tell the exact layout of the house, we can assume that if the back porch faces south, then the front porch could conceivably point north.

1. Label each of the rooms in the following layout of the Logan home.

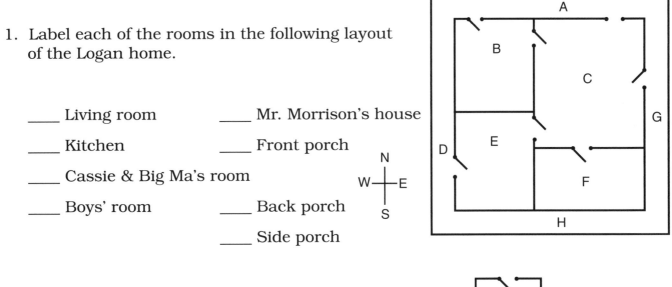

_____ Living room   _____ Mr. Morrison's house

_____ Kitchen   _____ Front porch

_____ Cassie & Big Ma's room

_____ Boys' room   _____ Back porch

                         _____ Side porch

2. Draw a layout of Cassie's classroom, identifying key objects in the room (refer to page 18).

Student Directives

1. Relate why Big Ma allowed Stacey & Cassie to accompany her to Strawberry.
2. Tell why Big Ma parks the wagon in the back of the field at the market.
3. Review Cassie's behavior at the mercantile.
4. Describe the events after Cassie bumps into Lillian Jean.
5. Discuss Cassie's feelings when she is made to apologize to Lillian Jean.

Vocabulary

warily	done very cautiously
wheedle	to get something by flattery or gentle urging
teeming	full of something
clabber	sour milk that has thickened or curdled
humiliate	put to shame; lower someone's dignity
retaliate	to get revenge
malevolent	harmful or evil; having intense hatred
falter	to move unsteadily or hesitate in speaking

Summary

Cassie and Stacey are allowed to go to the town of Strawberry on market day with Big Ma because Mr. Avery asked Big Ma to give T.J. a ride to the mercantile. When they arrive at the field where the market is held, Cassie wants to know why Big Ma parks the wagon in the back of the field. Big Ma explains that the entrance area is reserved for the "white folks." After market, Big Ma goes to see Mr. Jamison, the lawyer, and instructs the children to wait in the wagon till she gets back. But, T.J. talks the other two into going ahead to the mercantile. While Mr. Barnett is filling the Avery order, T.J. shows Stacey the pistol he'd like to get. The shop owner stops filling T.J.'s order to wait on some white customers. Cassie thinks Mr. Barnett has forgotten them, so she tries to remind him. Mr. Barnett insults Cassie and tells her to leave the store when she talks back to him. Once outside, as Stacey runs for Big Ma, Cassie absentmindedly backed into Lillian Jean Simms who wants an apology. She also orders Cassie to get down in the road. Cassie, of course, refuses to get off the sidewalk. Mr. Simms then pushes her down and orders her to not only apologize but also to refer to Lillian Jean as "Miz." Jeremy tries to stand up for Cassie, but his father glares angrily at him. When Big Ma arrives on the scene, she is afraid to put up a fuss with Mr. Simms. Reluctantly, she tells Cassie to apologize. This cruel day brought painful tears to Cassie's eyes.

Elements of a Narrative

Stories, whether they are short or the length of a novel, have certain main elements which make them easily read and understood, as well as interesting.

One of these main elements is the **characters**: the *people* the story is about. The author of a novel shows a character's personality by the things the character does, says, and thinks, as well as through description.

Another element is **setting**. It is the *where* and *when* of a story: the place and time a story takes place. The author may make this information very clear at the beginning of a story, or it may be left to the reader to gather it through inference.

The **conflict**(s) in a novel are those problems a character has with another character, with society, with nature, or even with himself or herself. The story largely centers around the conflict(s), which are often resolved by the end of the novel.

Plot is a very important part of a story. Plot is the events, or what happens in a story. The events in a book lead to a turning point for the characters and the plot usually continues, showing how the turning point affects the characters and their lives.

Elements of a Narrative & Outlining   Name _____

Directions: Study the basic elements from your reading so far. Complete the following outline.

Main Character

Describe Cassie.

A. _____

_____

B. _____

_____

C. _____

_____

Setting

Describe the place and time of the story.

A. Where: _____

_____

B. When: _____

_____

Conflicts

Describe the main problems with which the character deals.

A. _____

_____

B. _____

_____

C. _____

_____

Plot

From your reading so far, tell how you think the events will develop.

A. _____

_____

B. _____

_____

C. _____

Student Directives

1. Relate the surprise when Cassie and Stacey arrive home from market.

2. Review Uncle Hammer's response to Cassie's encounter with Mr. Simms and Lillian Jean.

3. Discuss Mrs. Logan's explanation to Cassie about white people's beliefs.

4. Tell about Stacey's early Christmas present.

5. Describe what happens when the Logans ride in Uncle Hammer's car after church.

Vocabulary

audible	loud enough to be heard
nattily	in a neat, trim, stylish manner
aloofness	standing apart; emotional distance
moping	in a dull, quiet, and sad mood; sulking
reprimand	severe criticism or scolding
reverently	very respectfully
spindly	long and thin and usually weak

Summary

When Big Ma, Stacey and Cassie return that night from the market, they discover a new Packard parked in their front yard which looks like Mr. Granger's. To their great delight, the car belongs to Uncle Hammer who's come for the Christmas season. Cassie immediately tells her uncle about her awful day, and how horribly she was treated by Mr. Simms and Lillian Jean. Big Ma and Mrs. Logan are fearful that Uncle Hammer will lose his temper and try to get revenge so they send Stacey to get Mr. Morrison who jumps into the Packard with Hammer as he speeds away. Mrs. Logan tries to tell Cassie why Big Ma made her apologize to Lillian Jean. She explains that some white people have to believe they are better than black people in order to feel big. Fortunately, Mr. Morrison was able to stop Uncle Hammer from going after Mr. Simms so they all get to ride to church in the Packard. Stacey gets his early Christmas present from his uncle: a new coat. But Stacey becomes self-conscious when T.J. acts unimpressed and begins to tease him. After church, Hammer takes the family for a ride to Strawberry. They come back by way of Soldiers Bridge, which is only wide enough for one vehicle at a time. Uncle Hammer forces the Wallaces, who believe the Packard is Mr. Granger's, to let the Logans go first. When they pass and the Wallaces discover who they are, Mrs. Logan becomes concerned and tells Hammer that one day they will have to pay for this.

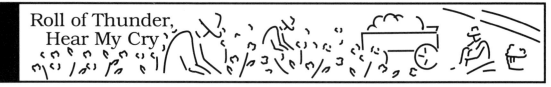

Sequencing

Name _____

Event 1: The Jefferson Davis bus sprays the Logans and Averys with dust on first day of school.

Event 2: _____

Event 3: _____

Event 4: _____

Event 5: _____

Event 6: Stacey gets caught with T.J.'s cheat notes and is punished.

Event 7: _____

Event 8: _____

Event 9: _____

Event 10: Cassie tells Mr. Barnett he is being unfair to T.J., Stacey, and her.

Event 11: _____

Event 12: _____

Event 13: _____

Event 14: _____

Event 15: _____

Directions: Organize the events from Chapters 1-6 in the order they occurred. Several have been completed for you.

- T.J. teases Stacey about his new coat.

- Logan kids make a "lake" in the road.

- Big Ma tells Cassie to do as Mr. Simms says.

- The Jefferson Davis bus sprays the Logans and Averys with dust on first day of school.

- Mrs. Logan takes her kids to visit the Berrys.

- Little Man refuses the textbook he is assigned.

- Cassie bumps into Lillian Jean.

- Uncle Hammer forces the Wallaces off the bridge.

- Uncle Hammer comes for Christmas.

- Stacey fights T.J. at the Wallace store.

- Mr. Logan brings Mr. Morrison home.

- Cassie tells Mr. Barnett he is being unfair to T.J., Stacey, and her.

- Cassie and Stacey go to market with Big Ma.

- Stacey gets caught with T.J.'s cheat notes and is punished.

- Cassie sees the night riders come to the house.

1. Mrs. Logan and Cassie discuss why Mr. Simms has to believe that white people are better than black people: to make himself feel big (page 127). Mr. Simms, like all of us, wants to feel important. What are some other things people believe to make themselves feel important or better than others? Do you believe, as Mrs. Logan does, that no one is better than anyone else? What, in your opinion, really makes someone important?

2. Mrs. Logan tells Cassie that the white people demand respect, but the black people really give them fear, not respect (page 129). To other black people, respect is given freely. What is the difference between respect and fear? Should people earn respect or be given it automatically? When is having fear appropriate (a wise thing to have)?

3. People have no choice about many things in life. Mrs. Logan names some of these on page 129, and reminds Cassie that we do have a choice over what we make of our lives. What are some things people do have control over? How does a person's attitude about life affect the choices a person can make and those he or she cannot?

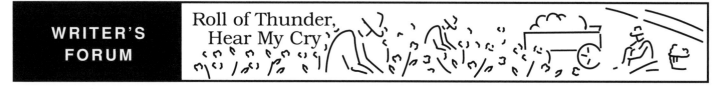

Issues: Writing About Yourself, Page 2   Name _____

T.J. takes Stacey and Cassie into Barnett's Mercantile while they wait for Big Ma. T.J. shows Stacey a pearl-handled hand-gun and says, "I'd sell my life for that gun."

1. Think about something you wanted very badly. What was it? Was having it worth "selling your life" as T.J. says? Did you get it? Why or why not? If not, do you still want it? If you did get it, is it still as important to you? Answer these questions in a paragraph.

2. Think about whether it is possible for people to want some material possession too much. Explain why you think so or not. Think about T.J. Do you believe he wants that gun too much? Predict what might happen if someone wants a material item enough to "sell his or her life" for it.

Mildred Taylor suggests a number of thought-provoking topics in *Roll of Thunder, Hear My Cry*. Choose one topic from the following list. Develop it by using examples and details from your own knowledge or experience.

1. Inequality between races in the South.

2. Strength and self-respect gained from receiving a good education.

3. Strength and courage gained by a loving family unit.

4. Importance of supporters when discrimination against a class or race of people is prevalent.

5. People who are so insecure that they can only feel important by putting down others.

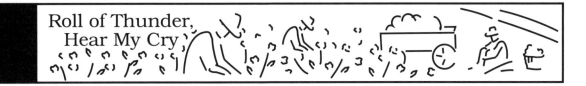
Name _____

Multiple Choice

Directions:

Circle the letter of the

correct answer.

1. Big Ma and Mama think there is something wrong with Cassie because

   A. she is restless in her sleep and stays indoors a lot.

   B. her head is hot.

   C. she starts to cry when the dish breaks.

2. The Logan land was once

   A. owned by a Louisiana family.

   B. worked by the Simms.

   C. Granger land.

3. Instead of whipping her children for going to the Wallace store, Mrs. Logan

   A. sends them to bed without dinner.

   B. wakes them early on Saturday to do extra work.

   C. takes them to see the man whom the Wallaces burned.

4. Stacey and Cassie are allowed to go to market because

   A. Big Ma needs their help.

   B. they will keep T.J. from bothering Big Ma.

   C. they have raised the eggs that will be sold.

5. At market, Big Ma parks the wagon at the back of the field because

   A. only men are allowed at the front.

   B. only people selling meat and vegetables are allowed at the front.

   C. only whites are allowed at the front.

6. Cassie reminds Mr. Barnett that he isn't finished with T.J.'s order

   A. because she thinks he's forgotten about them.

   B. in a rude manner.

   C. by stepping in front of the girl he was waiting on.

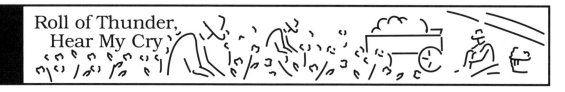
7. Big Ma makes Cassie apologize to Lillian Jean

   A. because Cassie was wrong.

   B. to avoid further trouble.

   C. because she was angry at Cassie.

8. Uncle Hammer's way of dealing with the injustice done to Cassie was to

   A. take a long walk.

   B. talk about the problem.

   C. angrily go for revenge.

9. Stacey's pleasure in his new wool coat is lessened because

   A. the coat is too big.

   B. T.J. teases him.

   C. he discovers a hole in the coat.

10. When Uncle Hammer forces the Wallaces off the bridge,

   A. Mrs. Logan is concerned about revenge.

   B. the Wallaces laugh at them.

   C. the Logan children are scared.

Vocabulary

Directions:

Fill in the blank with the correct word.

pact	malevolent	aloofness
expound	falter	reverently
vex	audible	reprimand
wheedle		

1. _____ loud enough to be heard

2. _____ agreement

3. _____ very respectfully

4. _____ to get something by flattery

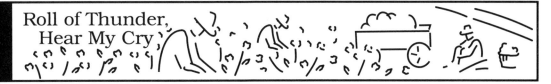
5. _____ severe criticism or scolding

6. _____ to explain or interpret

7. _____ harmful or evil; having intense hatred

8. _____ to bring trouble or wrong to; to annoy

9. _____ standing apart; emotional distance

10. _____ to move unsteadily or to hesitate in speaking

Essay Questions

Directions:

Answer in complete

sentences.

1. Describe T.J. Give examples from the story (things T.J. does and says) to help you show his personality in your paragraph about him._____

_____

_____

_____

2. Explain why, using what you've learned in the story so far, Stacey decides to confess to Mrs. Logan that he went to the Wallace store._____

_____

_____

_____

3. Explain why Mrs. Logan wants other families to stop shopping at the Wallace store._____

_____

_____

_____

Student Directives

1. Tell why Stacey gives his coat to T.J.
2. Relate how Uncle Hammer responds to Stacey "losing" his coat.
3. Review Stacey's conversation with his father concerning Jeremy.
4. Describe Mr. Jamison's visit.
5. Discuss Mr. Granger's threats to Mr. Logan.

Vocabulary

placid	calm; peaceful
eviction	forced out or expelled
revenue	money collected from rent or taxation
denote	to indicate a meaning; to symbolize
insolent	showing no respect for authority
impaled	made helpless as if pierced by a sharp object

Summary

T.J. has once again taken advantage of Stacey's insecurity. T.J. has managed to get the wool coat with the promise that he'll use it only until Stacey grows into it. Uncle Hammer will not allow Stacey to reclaim the coat. He says if Stacey's not smart enough to hold on to his possessions, then he doesn't deserve them. Cassie feels Hammer's "tongue-lashing" is worse that the "strap." The festive season begins with Mr. Logan's return on Christmas Eve when many stories pass among the adults. On Christmas Day, the Averys come over for a big dinner. And, Jeremy comes over, unknown to his family, to give Stacey a gift. Papa will not advise Stacey on whether he should keep the gift, but he does discourage a friendship with Jeremy because blacks and whites live in unequal circumstances. The day after Christmas, Big Ma signs the land over to her sons. While Mr. Jamison is at their home, he offers to back the credit for those families who want to shop in Vicksburg. He also warns them about Mr. Granger's intentions to get back at the Logans any way he can. When Mr. Jamison tells Mr. Logan that he won't really be able to beat the Wallaces or Mr. Granger, Mr. Logan says he wants his kids to know he tried. A few days later, Mr. Granger shows up after he learns that Mr. Logan, Uncle Hammer, and Mr. Morrison had gone to Vicksburg to shop for numerous families. He threatens that he'll do anything to stop their boycott of the Wallace store, including getting their loan called in and increasing his charges to his sharecroppers.

Comparison and Contrast

Name _____

Stacey's best friend is T.J. Stacey has a conversation with his father in which he admits that Jeremy could be a better friend than T.J. if Stacey would let him.

There are various qualities which make a good friend. In 1933, in Mississippi, there were also issues of reality that were considered, such as those Mr. Logan discusses with Stacey.

A. Complete the following lists, using information from the book about T.J. and Jeremy. What qualities would make each of them a good friend? What about each makes them less appealing as a friend to Stacey?

B. Think about yourself. What qualities do you have that make you a good friend? What do you consider before choosing a friend? List your considerations at the bottom or back of this page.

T.J.		Jeremy	
Good Friendship Quality	Difficult or Unappealing Quality or Issue	Good Friendship Quality	Difficult or Unappealing Quality or Issue

Student Directives

1. Tell what Cassie does to get revenge on Lillian Jean.
2. Relate how T.J. deals with failing Mrs. Logan's class.
3. Describe what happens when Mr. Granger and the other men visit Mrs. Logan's classroom.
4. Review T.J.'s actions at Wallace's store, and how his black friends regard him now.
5. Discuss T.J.'s reaction and comments when he realizes that the Logans are no longer his friends.

Vocabulary

fuming	showing irritation or building anger
feigned	pretended
barren	not fertile or productive
interjected	inserted or thrown in
bewildered	confused; filled with uncertainty
fallow	land left unseeded or without crops for a season

Summary

Cassie speaks to Papa about the issue with Lillian Jean. He tries to help her understand that there are some things that are best left alone because taking a stand might bring worse trouble. Cassie pretends to agree with Lillian Jean's view of her "place" in the world. She begins to carry Lillian Jean's books every day and in time learns of Lillian Jean's secrets. Only Stacey seems to know what Cassie is really up to and orders everyone, including T.J., to keep silent. Ultimately, Cassie finds the opportunity to get her revenge by luring Lillian Jean into the woods to beat her up. Cassie tells the surprised and stunned Lillian Jean that she'll disclose all her secrets if she tells. And, then, she makes Lillian Jean apologize. T.J., meanwhile, gets caught cheating on the final exams, and once again fails Mrs. Logan's class. Angrily, he runs away presumably to Wallace's store, claiming that Mrs. Logan failed him on purpose. Later, Mr. Wallace, Mr. Granger and another man from the school board come about complaints regarding Mrs. Logan's teaching methods. This encounter leads to Mrs. Logan getting fired. Later, a friend tells Stacey that T.J., while at the Wallace store, reported that Mrs. Logan is trying to get people to stop shopping there, and that she is destroying school property. T.J. denies having done this, but no one believes him anymore and he is shunned by the other students at Great Faith. T.J. pretends that he doesn't need Stacey or the other kids because he has new friends and they are white.

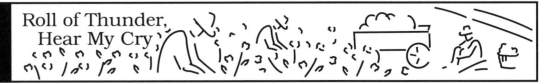

Cause and Effect

Name _____

Directions: On the left is a list of causes. On the right is a list of effects. Match the correct effect with its cause by placing the correct letter in the blank.

A **CAUSE** produces a result	An **EFFECT** results from a cause

1. Because Little Man did not want to dirty his clothes by climbing up the bank, _____

2. Mrs. Logan doesn't think the black students should get old books, so _____

3. Because Mr. Logan worries about his family when he's away working on the railroad, _____

4. The Logan children dig a ditch in the road _____

5. The Wallaces are cruel to the community's black citizens, so _____

6. Because Cassie causes Mr. Barnett trouble, _____

7. Uncle Hammer has a quick temper and _____

8. Since Stacey lets T.J. fool him into giving away his new coat, _____

9. When the Logan children go to the Wallace store against instructions, _____

10. When T.J. betrays the Logans by talking negatively about Mrs. Logan, _____

A. he brings Mr. Morrison home to work and stay with the Logan family.

B. Mrs. Logan encourages families not to shop at their store.

C. he wants to immediately go after Mr. Simms for pushing Cassie.

D. they are whipped by Mr. Logan.

E. he got even dirtier when the bus went by.

F. and the Jefferson Davis bus breaks down, making it useless and unable to splash mud.

G. he is no longer treated as a friend by the students.

H. Uncle Hammer won't let him take it back.

I. she puts new pages in the front of the text books.

J. he tells her to never return.

Student Directives

1. Tell what the Logans learn about T.J.'s new "friends."
2. Discuss Mrs. Logan's explanation of T.J.'s problem.
3. Review the standing of the boycott against the Wallaces at this point.
4. Describe what happens to Mr. Logan, Mr. Morrison, and Stacey on the way from Vicksburg.
5. Relate Stacey's feelings about this incident.

Vocabulary

lingered	slow to leave
amenities	something that makes life more pleasant
lilt	lively rhythm
rile	to anger or upset
premature	happening before the usual time
agitated	disturbed or excited
prod	to urge into action

Summary

The Logans learn that Jeremy's brothers laugh at T.J. behind his back. When Cassie says he must be "dumb" to believe his new "friends" like him, Mrs. Logan explains that T.J. wants attention so he puts up with the abuse. Meanwhile, Mr. Jamison reports to Mr. Logan that the Wallaces are talking about putting a stop to the people who are trying to ruin their business. Some of the families are pulling out of the boycott because of threats from Mr. Granger, Mr. Montier, and the Wallaces. Mr. Logan talks to Stacey and Cassie about not giving up, but also about being understanding when others feel they must. Mr. Logan and Mr. Morrison decide to go to Vicksburg again in spite of Mrs. Logan's worries. This time they take Stacey, partly because Papa wants Stacey to learn how to handle business and partly because he is worried about the possible influence of T.J.'s unruly behavior. Mrs. Logan's worries come to pass when the men do not come home till very late, and she learns that Mr. Logan has been injured. The men had been attacked by three white men but Mr. Morrison was able to beat up two of them: they were Wallaces. Stacey relates to Cassie and his brothers that the back wheels fell off after having been intentionally loosened. Papa was shot while trying to reset the first wheel which made the mule bolt, and the wagon ran over Papa's leg. Stacey reveals that he feels responsible because he couldn't hold the mule.

Conflict

In *Roll of Thunder, Hear My Cry*, Stacey deals with a struggle within himself. This is called an internal conflict. Jeremy wants to be Stacey's friend, but Stacey is undecided whether he should encourage a friendship because of the trouble it could bring. Jeremy tells Stacey that he likes him and his family. He likes to walk part way to school with them and he brings Stacey a handmade Christmas gift. Stacey likes Jeremy and admits that he would be a better friend than T.J. Stacey also knows that, because they are different races, neither of their fathers approve of a friendship.

Using the above information from the story and your work from the Chapter Seven Skill Page, *Compare and Contrast*, to support your advice, write a letter to Stacey in which you show that you understand how he might be feeling as he thinks about this problem. Reference your own personal situation when you had to make an important decision regarding your choice of a friend.

Did your parents ever disapprove of one of your friends? Did you understand your parents reasons? How did you deal with the problem? How did you decide or finally solve the problem?

Then, tell Stacey what you think he should do. (Note: Your letter might include information on how the world is more tolerant of inter-racial friendships now, some background on the civil rights movement of the 1950s, or a friend of yours who is not of your race.)

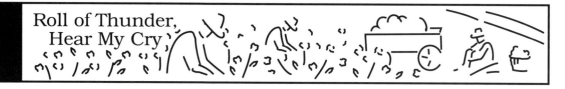

Multiple Choice

Directions:

Circle the letter of the correct answer.

1. Mr. Morrison's parents

    A. were from the same county as the Logans.

    B. were killed by night men.

    C. left Mr. Morrison with relatives when he was a boy and moved away to find work.

2. Big Ma signs the land over to

    A. Papa and Uncle Hammer.

    B. the four Logan children.

    C. Mr. and Mrs. Logan.

3. Mr. Jamison

    A. is asked but refuses to back the credit in Vicksburg.

    B. is a good friend of Harlan Granger's.

    C. tries to do what he can to help the black people.

4. When Cassie starts carrying Lillian Jean's books,

    A. everyone is relieved that Cassie has learned her place.

    B. Stacey tells Mrs. Logan.

    C. Stacey seems to understand Cassie's plan.

5. Mr. Logan tells Cassie that

    A. there are some things you must take a stand on.

    B. she should never get mad.

    C. Lillian Jean should apologize to Cassie.

6. Mrs. Logan was fired

    A. because she had been teaching too long in Spokane County.

    B. when Mr. Granger and other white men visit her classroom.

    C. because her students weren't learning enough.

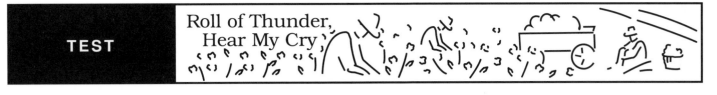

7. Stacey doesn't beat up T.J. when Mrs. Logan is fired because he

   A. knows T.J. has enough punishment coming.

   B. is going to wait for the right moment.

   C. feels sorry for T.J.

8. Mr. Logan needs to return to the railroad

   A. and he is looking forward to going.

   B. to pay the taxes and mortgage on the land.

   C. and Mr. Morrison will be going with him.

9. Mr. Logan wants to take Stacey to Vicksburg because he

   A. needs Stacey's help.

   B. is afraid he'll get into trouble at home.

   C. wants to teach him how to handle things and to be strong.

10. Stacey thinks Mr. Logan's broken leg is his fault because he

   A. disobeyed his father.

   B. wasn't strong enough to hold the mule.

   C. wanted to hurry home.

Vocabulary

Directions:

Fill in the blank with the correct word.

goaded	fuming	lilt
placid	bewildered	rile
eviction	fallow	agitated
impaled		

1. _____ to make helpless as if pierced by a sharp object

2. _____ filled with uncertainty; confused

3. _____ stirred to action

4. _____ disturbed or excited

5. _____ lively rhythm

6. _____ forced out or expelled

7. _____ land left unseeded or without crops for a season

8. _____ to anger or upset

9. _____ calm; peaceful

10. _____ showing irritation or building anger

Essay Questions

Directions:

Answer in complete

sentences.

1. What is the principle which Uncle Hammer shares with Stacey after Stacey gives his new coat away? In paragraph form, describe it in your own words and then explain why you agree or disagree._____

_____

_____

_____

2. Explain why T.J.'s actions caused him to lose his friends.

_____

_____

_____

Student Directives

1. Review what takes place when Mr. Morrison and the children return from the Wiggins' place.

2. Describe how the Logan children spend their August days after chores are done.

3. Tell Mr. Morrison's news when he returns from the bank in Strawberry.

4. Relate how the Logans pay off the mortgage completely.

5. Discuss how T.J. hopes to impress old friends at the church revival.

Vocabulary

lethargic	sluggish; moving without energy
amble	a slow, easy way of walking
complex	hard to understand or explain; complicated
reproach	scold, blame, or rebuke
sweltering	suffering with oppressive, intense heat
en masse	as a whole; altogether
desolate	abandoned; deprived of friendship

Summary

Mr. and Mrs. Logan continue to worry about finances when Mr. Morrison asks permission to take the planter over to Mr. Wiggins so he can plant some summer corn. Cassie and her brothers get to go on this happy excursion on this very fine day. The return trip is not as pleasant, though, when Kaleb Wallace screeches his beat-up truck to a halt right in front of the wagon and mule. Kaleb threatens Mr. Morrison, who calmly uses his brute strength to move the truck to the side of the road. Mrs. Logan is understandably upset when she is told this story. The Logan children, however, go down to the pond on these hot August days, not overly concerned about the trouble with the Wallaces. They sometimes meet Jeremy who keeps them informed about T.J. Meanwhile the fear of losing the land takes a turn for the worse when Mr. Morrison goes to pay the August installment on the loan. The bank sends a note recalling the loan. Payment in full is expected immediately. Mr. Logan calls Uncle Hammer for money. He sells his car and personally brings the money to Papa the first day of the Revival. On the last night of the Revival, T.J. brings the Simms' brothers. He brags about what they do for him, but none of his old friends are impressed. T.J. seems dejected, but goes with the Simms boys because they have promised to get him the pistol he wants.

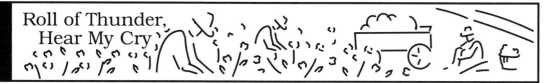

Figurative Language: Colloquialisms Name _____

A **colloquialism** is an expression used in informal conversation, often characteristic of a particular region. Mildred D. Taylor uses colloquialisms throughout *Roll of Thunder, Hear My Cry* to show everyday speech in this Mississippi rural setting. For instance: when Miss Crocker asks Cassie, "Do you want part of this switch?" (p.26), she is really asking Cassie if she's asking for a whipping.

Directions: Read the colloquialisms below and then write their literal meaning.

---

1. "...Big Ma had gone to a sick house..." (p. 9)

2. "...Mr. Berry was low sick..." (p.9)

3. "...I hear tells..." (p. 40)

4. "...I'm gonna wear y'all out." (p. 41)

5. "...he swung a mean switch." (p. 41)

6. "...he lit outa here..." (p. 82)

7. "Just worryin' me 'bout this land..." (p. 88)

8. "I wouldn't've done her that way." (p. 118)

9. "I hope he knocks his block off." (p. 125)

10. "Cassie, you cracked?" (p.171)

11. "...boy, you're a story." (p.230)

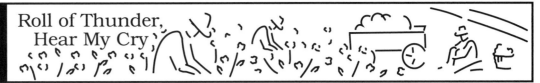
Identifying Characters

Name _____

Directions: Use the following list to choose the character who said the quote. Names can be used more than once.

Cassie	Mr. Logan	T.J.	Stacey
Big Ma	Mr. Granger	Christopher-John	Uncle Hammer
Lillian Jean	Little Man	Mr. Morrison	Jeremy
Mrs. Logan	Mr. Jamison		

_____ 1. "Y'all go ahead and get dirty if y'all wanna. Me, I'm gonna stay clean." (p. 4)

_____ 2. "Maybe I ought not tell y'all. It might hurt y'all's little ears." (p. 9)

_____ 3. "Cassie, you start up again and I'm sending you to the kitchen to study." (p. 59)

_____ 4. "All I wanted to do was eat my lunch!" (p. 63)

_____ 5. "But Papa told me to help you!" (p. 64)

_____ 6. "You sure are takin' a sorrowful long time to churn that butter." (p.69)

_____ 7. "Friends gotta trust each other...'cause ain't nothin' like a true friend." (p. 77)

_____ 8. "Don't need him here. All that work he doing, I could've done it myself." (p. 78)

_____ 9. "'Cause I'm leaving it up to you to tell her." (p. 87)

_____ 10. "He don't know nothin' 'bout me or this land, he think I'm gonna sell!" (p. 95)

_____ 11. "And you ought not be waiting on everybody 'fore you wait on us." (p. 111)

_____ 12. "Ah, let her pass...she ain't done nothin' to you." (p. 114)

_____ 13. "Ever since you went down into Louisiana to get Papa last summer you think you know so doggone much!" (p. 118)

_____ 14. "Got me a good mind to burn that place out." (p. 138)

_____ 15. "I'm a Southerner, born and bred, but that doesn't mean I approve of all that goes on here..." (p. 161)

_____ 16. "...I plan to do whatever I need to, to keep peace down in here." (p. 169)

_____ 17. "You plan on getting this land, you're planning on the wrong thing." (p. 170)

_____ 18. ...ain't no way I can afford to fail them things again." (p. 173)

_____ 19. "You're a lot like me,...but you got yourself a bad temper..." (p. 175)

_____ 20. "But, Cassie, why? You was such a nice little girl...." (p. 181)

Student Directives

1. Tell why T.J. goes to the Logan's late at night.
2. Review what the men who go to the Avery's intend to do.
3. Describe how Mr. Jamison tries to help.
4. Discuss Mr. Granger's attitude about the situation.
5. Relate the promise Cassie requires from Stacey before she takes the other boys home.

Vocabulary

despicable	deserving to be scorned
vulnerability	easily hurt
hastened	hurried
interminable	endless
akimbo	position of arms as if hands on hips
rasped	to make a harsh sound
emitted	sent forth
prone	likely to be or act a certain way

Summary

The muggy hot night threatens rain and keeps Cassie from sleeping. She hears a tapping on the porch which turns out to be T.J. He is badly injured and asks Stacey for help getting home. Stacey insists on knowing what happened, so T.J. tells the story: He went to Barnett's Mercantile with R.W. and Melvin Simms. T.J., believing they're just going to get the pistol and pay for it later, climbs through a window to open the door. The Simms' boys, their faces disguised, enter and proceed to rob the store. Mr. and Mrs. Barnett come down the stairs and they are injured by the Simms' boys in a struggle. They, then, beat up T.J. to keep him from talking. The Logan children escort T.J. home, and as they leave to return home, they notice the Simms', Wallace's and other whites show up. They throw the Averys out of the house and beat them while they try to find T.J. From their hiding place, the Logan children watch as Mr. Jamison drives up and tells the white men to let the law handle it. The sheriff arrives with the message that Mr. Granger wants no hanging on his property. But, the white men say they'll take T.J. somewhere else. They intend to hang T.J., and threaten to get Mr. Morrison and Mr. Logan, too. As Stacey sends Cassie, Christopher-John, and Little Man to get Papa, Cassie makes Stacey promise he'll not go down to the Avery's by himself. The thunder and lightening get worse as they run home.

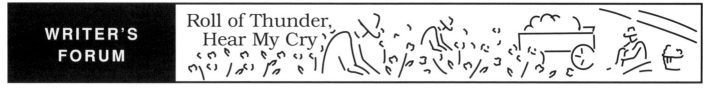

Creative Writing: Poetry

Name _____

Chapter 11 begins with a poem. The author has used the first two lines for the title of this book. Poetry can say something powerful in only a few words. Whereas it takes the whole book to tell one year in the life of Cassie Logan, these few lines of poetry tell a lot about many years in the lives of black people before slavery was outlawed.

Poems do not always have to rhyme, but they should have a meter or rhythm. Songs are often poems set to music. Poems can be short, or they can be long as the epic poem. They can have powerful meaning or be quite frivolous.

1. Why do you think Mildred Taylor chose the first two lines of this poem for the title of her book?

2. What kind of life do you think is depicted in this poem?

3. Is there any hope for a better life in this poem? Identify the passage which supports or does not support a better future.

Sometimes real dangers (fire, thunder, rain) are substituted in poetry for emotions. Try to imagine what feelings certain words bring to your mind (fire = danger; thunder = strength; rain = relief).

4. Tell about a poem or song you've heard which makes you feel strong emotions—i.e., hatred, love, fear.

5. Write a short poem about a dramatic incident in your life. Substitute concrete nouns (i.e, clouds) for abstract nouns (i.e., memories) as often as possible.

Student Directives

1. Relate Mrs. Logan's attitude about stopping the men from hanging T.J.
2. Describe what happens to the cotton.
3. Review what ends up happening to T.J.
4. Tell what Mr. Jamison warns Mr. Logan about.
5. Discuss the things Cassie thinks about after the fire is out and everyone returns home.

Vocabulary

traipsing	walking or traveling about
menacingly	in a threatening or dangerous manner
billow	to rise and roll in large waves
glint	a gleam or sparkle
acrid	sharp or bitter in taste or odor
oblivious	unaware
wan	having a pale or sickly color

Summary

When Cassie and her two younger brothers arrive home, their parents are ready to punish them. When Cassie reveals what has taken place at the Averys, Mr. Logan gets his gun and prepares to stop the hanging. Mrs. Logan begs him to find a way without using the gun. The tension of waiting after Mr. Logan and Mr. Morrison leave is interrupted when Mrs. Logan smells smoke and discovers the cotton is burning. Mrs. Logan and Big Ma go to fight the fire, instructing Cassie and the boys to stay home. Near dawn, Jeremy drops by and tells them what's happening in the field. As he is leaving, the hoped-for rain begins to fall. Cassie and Little Man decide they have to see the cotton field for themselves. They see blacks and whites working together to put out the fire. Cassie and Little Man return home just before Mama and learn that T.J. has been taken into Strawberry by the sheriff and Mr. Jamison. While the younger boys are being taken to bed, Cassie pleads with Stacey to tell what happened after she left. He tells her that the whites were just about to take T.J. away when the fire came up and Mr. Granger ordered everyone to fight it. Mr. Morrison then found Stacey and they went to fight the fire, too. Mr. Jamison comes by just as Papa and Mr. Morrison return. He reports that Mr. Barnett has died and that it is best if Mr. Logan stays clear of the whole situation. Cassie now realizes that Papa intentionally set the fire to stop the hanging. Later, alone in bed, Cassie cries about T.J. and the events of the night. She knows life will go on and be okay for her family, but not for T.J.

Plot Development

Organization of the plot is crucial to the success of a novel, and is often the most difficult to develop. As the story progresses, the plot moves toward a turning point, or climax. It can be pictured as a hill with the climax as the summit. The action "rises" as the reader gains more information and the conflicts are developed, all leading to the high point (climax). This high point is the event that changes the character's behavior or attitude. It is what the action has been rising toward. The result of this climax, which is called falling action, follows. This is where the changes happen. The falling action ends with the resolution, or final solving of the conflicts. The plot organization is more easily understood when it is set on an organization map (see map on following page).

Duplicate the Plot Organization Map on oversize paper for ease of student use.

Directions: Plot the events in the order they occur in the story.

•Mr. Jamison tries to stop hanging

•Jeremy brings Stacey a gift

•Mrs. Logan pastes new pages in the textbooks

•Cassie cries for T.J. and the land.

•Mrs. Logan is fired

•Big Ma makes Cassie apologize to Lillian Jean

•Papa brings Mr. Morrison

•Papa starts cotton on fire

•T.J. fails exams and talks about Mrs. Logan

•Logan kids dig a lake in the road

•The mortgage is called in

•T.J.'s family is thrown around when men want to hang T.J.

•Mr. Logan is injured.

•T.J. is taken to town to await punishment

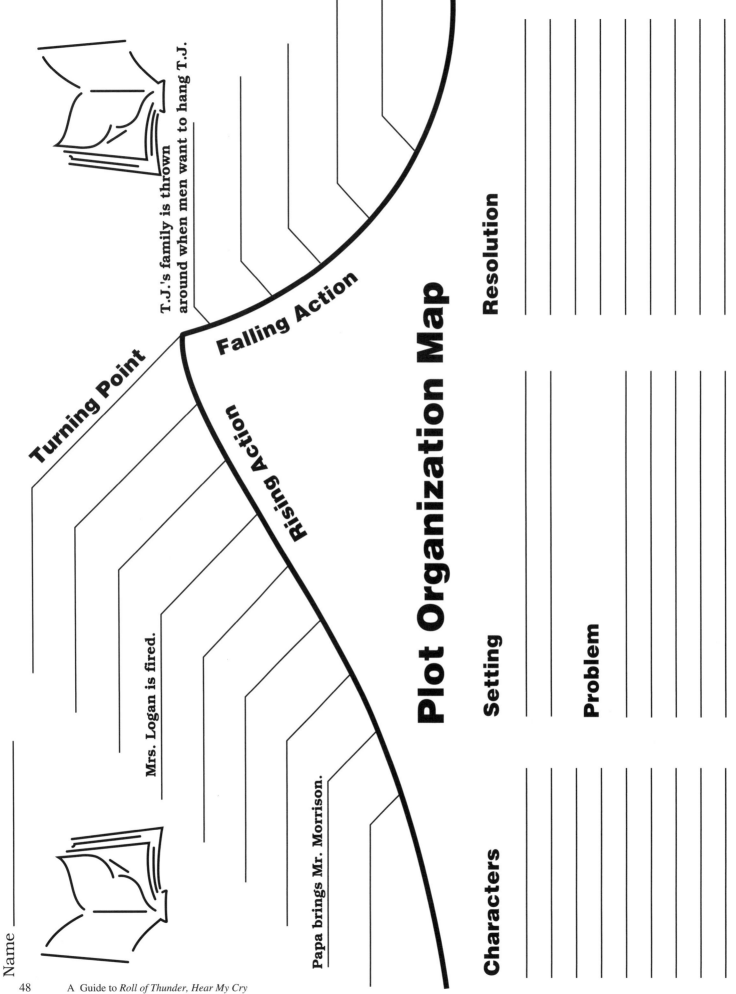

Plot Organization Map

Turning Point

Falling Action

Rising Action

T.J.'s family is thrown around when men want to hang T.J.

Mrs. Logan is fired.

Papa brings Mr. Morrison.

Setting

Resolution

Characters

Problem

Character Development

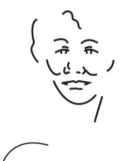

The Logan family and some of the other characters in *Roll of Thunder, Hear My Cry* display many virtues. For example, Mr. and Mrs. Logan model honest and responsible behavior to their children, who in turn try to live out the principles they've been taught.

When we read literature, we are not only entertained, but we learn. Included in the knowledge we gain is how to become strong in character. Being a virtuous character enriches our lives and the lives of those around us. *Roll of Thunder, Hear My Cry* gives us many good examples of how practicing character virtues can make our lives better.

The Discovering Literature Series focuses on ten character virtues:

Responsibility	Friendship
Courage	Persistence
Compassion	Hard Work
Loyalty	Self-Discipline
Honesty	Faith

The following pages highlight these character virtues. Using examples from your reading, find characters which embody these virtues.

Roll of Thunder,
Hear My Cry

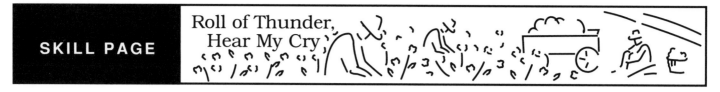

Character Development, Page 1

Name _____

Directions: Choose a character(s) from *Roll of Thunder, Hear My Cry* who possesses the virtue listed and briefly explain, using examples from the book, how that character displays that virtue.

Responsibility

_____
character

_____
_____
_____
_____

Courage

_____
character

_____
_____
_____
_____

Compassion

_____
character

_____
_____
_____
_____

Loyalty

_____
character

_____
_____
_____
_____

Honesty

_____
character

_____
_____
_____
_____

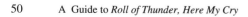

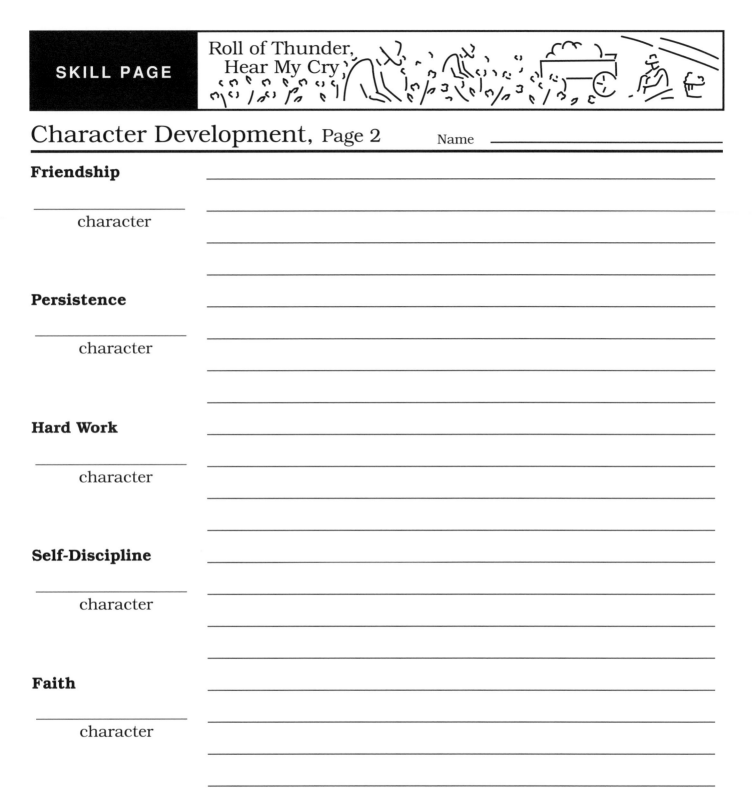

Character Development, Page 2   Name _____

Friendship

_____
character

_____

_____

_____

_____

Persistence

_____
character

_____

_____

_____

_____

Hard Work

_____
character

_____

_____

_____

_____

Self-Discipline

_____
character

_____

_____

_____

_____

Faith

_____
character

_____

_____

_____

_____

Which virtue or virtues do you think best typify Cassie's strong character. Justify your answers.

_____

_____

_____

_____

_____

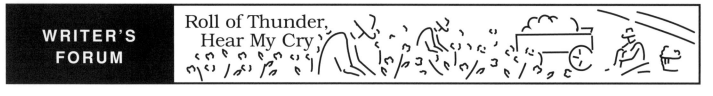

Round and Flat Characters

Name _____

A round character is one which is fully developed physically, emotionally, intellectually, and spiritually, such as Huck Finn or Tom Sawyer. A round character includes the main player (the hero or heroine, the protagonist) and well-developed subordinate players (friend, brother, pet). Readers know almost everything about the main character: his or her hand gestures, thinking, patterns of behavior. A round character is 3-dimensional (multi-faceted).

A flat character is 1-dimensional, and often stereotypical such as Cinderella's fairy godmother or her stepmother. Flat characters have lesser importance in a story. They are used to help readers create certain specific images without the writers needing to invest a lot of time to develop them. Flat characters are never main characters. Instead, they play supporting roles which affect the main character's growth either positively or negatively.

1. Next to each character in the following list, write "R" for round or "F" for flat.

Cassie	Mr. Jamison	Big Ma
Jeremy	Stacey	Mr. Barnett
T.J.	Mr. Granger	Mr. Morrison
Lillian Jean	Little Man	Claude
Mr. Simms	Christopher-John	

2. For those characters you've decided are "round," cite passages from the book to support your decision.

3. Decide upon one of the above characters which you believe to be "flat" and "round" him or her out. Develop the character into a more 3-dimensional person.

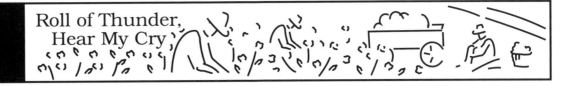

Multiple Choice

Directions:

Circle the letter of the

correct answer.

1. Jeremy tells the Logan children that his brothers
   A. seem to be very fond of T.J.
   B. talk about T.J. behind his back.
   C. treat him (Jeremy) better lately.

2. Mr. Logan doesn't want to call Hammer unless they really need money because
   A. he doesn't want to bother Hammer.
   B. Mr. Logan wants to pay his own bills.
   C. Mr. Logan is afraid Hammer will get into trouble with his temper.

3. T.J. brings the Simms brothers to the church during the revival
   A. to prove to his old friends that the Simms' are his new friends.
   B. in hopes of getting them to stay for the services.
   C. to ask if anyone needed anything from the store.

4. To prove he's telling the truth, T.J. admits to
   A. trying to find test answers.
   B. telling a lie about Cassie.
   C. telling on Mrs. Logan.

5. All the Logan kids take T.J. home because
   A. Stacey is afraid to go alone.
   B. Cassie and the other boys don't want to be left behind.
   C. Stacey doesn't want the others to wake up their parents.

6. The men who come for T.J. also threaten to kill
   A. Mr. and Mrs. Avery.
   B. Mr. Jamison, Mr. Morrison, and Mr. Logan.
   C. Mr. and Mrs. Logan.

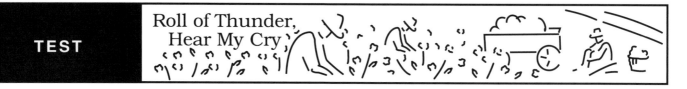
7. When Cassie, Christopher-John, and Little Man get home,

A. everyone is asleep.

B. Mr. Logan is ready to whip them.

C. Big Ma doesn't believe their story.

8. Mrs. Logan wants Mr. Logan to

A. send Mr. Morrison for Stacey.

B. forget about T.J.

C. find a way to help T.J. without endangering himself.

9. Big Ma and Mrs. Logan go to fight the fire with

A. burlap sacks and a wash tub.

B. hoses and shovels.

C. buckets and burlap sacks.

10. Mr. Logan tells Cassie and Stacey that

A. T.J. will be fine.

B. T.J. is guilty.

C. he wishes he could lie about T.J.

Vocabulary

Directions:

Fill in the blank with the correct word.

acrid   hastened   adamant

oblivious   emitted   reproach

traipsing   rasped   amble

interminable

1. _____ scold, blame, or rebuke

2. _____ endless

3. _____ to make a harsh sound

4. _____ sharp or bitter in taste or odor

5. _____ not giving in

6. _____ hurried

7. _____ walking or traveling about

8. _____ a slow, easy way of walking

9. _____ sent forth

10. _____ unaware

Essay Questions

Directions:

Answer in complete

sentences.

1. Cassie says that Stacey feels a responsibility for T.J. and that possibly it's because Stacey thinks even someone as despicable as T.J. needs a friend. Do you think Stacey might feel this way? Give some examples from the story to support your answer. Also, tell what you believe: do even "despicable" people need friends? Why or why not?

_____

_____

_____

2. To put out the fire, everyone, black and white, men and women, worked side by side. What do you think the author wants you to learn about people from this incident? Why doesn't this type of working together happen more often?

_____

_____

_____

3. Through Cassie's experiences, what have you learned about being a black person in the South during the 1930s?

_____

_____

_____

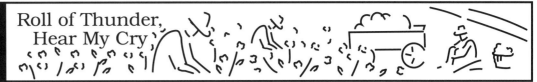

Chapter Title_____ Name_____

Chapter Summary: _____

_____

_____

_____

_____

_____

_____

 _____

_____

_____

_____

_____

_____

_____

Chapter Vocabulary:

1. _____

_____

_____

2. _____

_____

3. _____

_____

4. _____

_____

5. _____

_____

NAME: _____

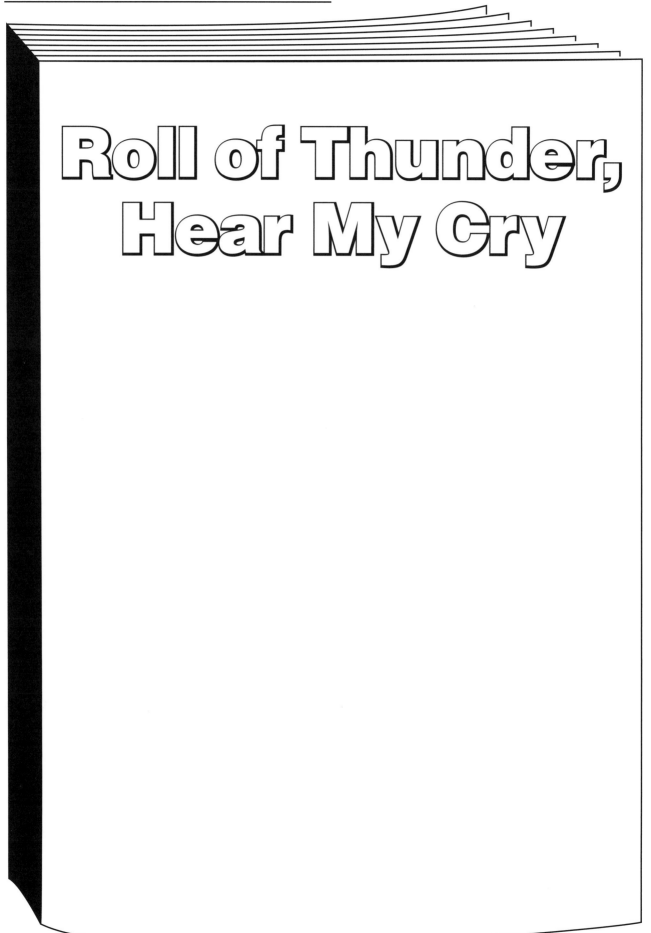

Roll of Thunder, Hear My Cry

Skill Page: About the Characters. p. 10

Character Chart

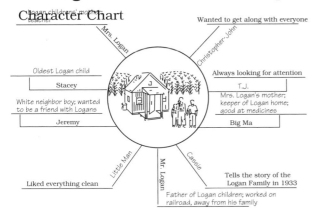

Logan children's mother; teacher — Mrs. Logan

Wanted to get along with everyone — Christopher-John

Oldest Logan child — Stacey

Always looking for attention — T.J.

White neighbor boy; wanted to be a friend with Logans — Jeremy

Mrs. Logan's mother; keeper of Logan home; good at medicines — Big Ma

Liked everything clean — Little Man

Mr. Logan — Father of Logan children; worked on railroad, away from his family

Tells the story of the Logan Family in 1933 — Cassie

Skill Page: Setting, p.12

1. "Now it was 1933..." (p.7)
2. "...on a bright August-like October morning..." (p.4) or "...school adjusted terms accordingly, beginning in October..." (p.16)
3. "...when the cotton was planted..."(p.16)
4. "In 1930 the price of cotton dropped. ...Papa set out looking for work,... (p.7)

Skill Page: Fig. Language - Similes, p. 14

1. dust / snow
   Both fall slowly and evenly.
2. road / serpent
   Both wind back and forth (not a straight line).
3. bus / dragon
   Both blowing out some substance as if angry.
4. Miss Crocker / giant
   Miss Crocker is compared to a giant because she is so much bigger than Little Man.
5. Little Man / wounded animal
   Both jump as if injured.
6. rain / hail
   The rain is compared to hail because it is falling heavily.
7. headlights / cat eyes
   Both shine at night and are the only part visible.
8. Mr. Morrison / jungle cat
   Both move quietly and purposefully.

Writer's Forum: What Do You Think? p. 15

Accept reasonable answers in good English essay form.

Test, Chapters 1-3, p. 16

Multiple Choice

1. B	6. C
2. A	7. A
3. C	8. B
4. C	9. B
5. B	10. C

Vocabulary

1. temerity	6. undaunted
2. penetrating	7. scoff
3. precariously	8. penchant
4. resiliency	9. relent
5. admonish	10. fibrous

Essay Questions

1. The Logans believe they are just as important as anyone of any other race, so they do not teach their children to just accept the way things are as though inequality is right. Examples: Mrs. Logan thinks the students deserve better than books which are old and unwanted. She fixes them to make them seem nicer for her kids and her students; the Logans teach their children not to patronize stores where blacks are treated badly; Big Ma tries to encourage Little Man not to let the ignorant white people on the bus upset him.

2. Jeremy is different because he is the only white child who associates with blacks. He is sincere, but they are suspicious of him and don't let him get too close in friendship. The whites shun and beat him because he associates with blacks. He looks like the world is slung around his neck because he knows the whites' treatment of blacks is wrong and can do nothing about it and it probably hurts him that the blacks don't trust him either.

Accept reasonable answers.

Skill Page: Understanding Directions, p. 21

C - Living room	I - Mr. Morrison's house
F - Kitchen	A - Front porch
B - Cassie and Big Ma's room	H - Back Porch
E - Boys' room	D, G - Side porches

Skill Page: Narrative & Outlining, p. 23

Main Character - Cassie

A. Feisty; speaks her mind
B. Loves her family
C. Respects her parents and Big Ma and wants to do right

Setting

A. Where: Spokane County, Mississippi
B. When: 1933

Conflicts

A. Blacks vs. whites: the community has not accepted its black citizens as equal
B. Logan children vs. the Jefferson Davis bus: they try to avoid it to keep from getting sprayed with dust or mud
C. Black community vs. Wallaces: Wallace's store provides activities which are a bad influence on the children; the Wallaces themselves are cruel
D. T.J. vs. self: too lazy to study, he causes trouble

Plot

A. Great Faith school has begun a new year
B. The night riders have been treating blacks cruelly
C. Papa brings Mr. Morrison to live at their farm
D. The Logan children "fix" the road in order to incapacitate the Jefferson Davis bus
E. Stacey fights T.J. at the Wallace store
F. Logans visit the Berrys and Mrs. Logan encourages people to stay away from the Wallaces

Accept reasonable answers.

Skill Page: Sequencing, p.26

Event 1:   The Jefferson Davis bus sprays the Logans and Averys with dust on the first day of school.
Event 2:   Little Man refuses the textbook he is assigned.
Event 3:   Mr. Logan brings Mr. Morrison home.
Event 4:   Logan kids make a "lake" in the road.
Event 5:   Cassie sees the night riders come to the house.
Event 6:   Stacey gets caught with T.J.'s cheat notes and is punished.
Event 7:   Stacey fights T.J. at the Wallace store.
Event 8:   Mrs. Logan takes her kids to visit the Berrys.
Event 9:   Cassie and Stacey go to market with Big Ma.
Event 10: Cassie tells Mr. Barnett he is being unfair to T.J., Stacey, and her.
Event 11: Cassie bumps into Lillian Jean.
Event 12: Big Ma tells Cassie to do as Mr. Simms says.
Event 13: Uncle Hammer comes for Christmas.
Event 14: T.J. teases Stacey about his new coat.
Event 15: Uncle Hammer forces the Wallaces off the bridge.

Writer's Forum: Issues...about yourself, p. 27

(partial answers)

Possible responses to the question:

1. What are some other things people believe to make themselves feel important?
   Having money makes you important.
   Having clothes of a popular style makes you important.
   Being popular makes you important.
   Owning a nice car makes you important.
   Winning contests makes you important.
   Being good at sports makes you important.

2. When is having fear appropriate (a wise thing to have)?
   When it causes you to be careful. Examples: on a busy street, near a river, around an unfamiliar animal, when making an important decision.

3. What are some things people do have control over?
   Whether we are going to be fair and honest to others, whether we will work hard, what kind of friends we will be to others.

Test, Chapters 4-6, p. 29

Multiple Choice

1. A	6. A
2. C	7. B
3. C	8. C
4. B	9. B
5. C	10. A

Vocabulary

1. audible	6. expound
2. pact	7. malevolent
3. reverently	8. vex
4. wheedle	9. aloofness
5. reprimand	10. falter

Essay Questions

1. T.J. is always trying to get away with something. He talks a lot and talks fast and knows how to get people's attention, which he is always seeking. T.J. will blame anyone for something he's done if he can get away with it. He likes nice things, but doesn't seem very willing to work.

   Possible examples: blames Claude for going to Wallace store and Claude gets in trouble; brags to the Logan kids that he knows how to get out of work; tries to get Stacey to sneak answers to the test and then tries to sneak them himself; makes cheat notes and lets Stacey take blame when they are noticed; wants the gun and says he would sell his life for it; teases Stacey about his new coat when really he is jealous.

2. Stacey wants to show Mrs. Logan that he is a man. He offers Mrs. Logan help when trouble comes and he believes at first that Mr. Morrison is not needed at their home because he could take care of whatever problems there might be. When Mr. Morrison tells him it is up to him to tell Mrs. Logan about going to the Wallace store, Stacey understands that as a mature man, he would be honest and so he is.

3. The Wallace business will hurt with the loss of customers. It will send the message to the Wallaces that others know they are doing wrong in the community, and that the black community will not put up with it. Mrs. Logan wants people to stand together because she knows this can make them successful.

Accept reasonable answers.

Skill Page: Comparison and Contrast, p. 33

	T.J.			Jeremy	
Good Friendship Quality	Difficult or Unappealing Quality or Issue	Good Friendship Quality	Difficult or Unappealing Quality or Issue
Same race	Lets others take the blame (lets both Claude and Stacey take his punishment)	Loyal (doesn't care that others make fun of him for associating with blacks)	Different race
Families are friends	Uses people (tricks Stacey out of his new coat)	Tries to stand up for Cassie in Strawberry	
	Cheats on tests	Generous (brings gifts to Logans and Stacey)	Stacey doesn't know if Jeremy will remain a friend as he gets older
	Lets others do the work	Concerned (when the bus splatters the Logans)	
	Always wants attention		

Skill Page: Cause and Effect, p. 35

1. E	6. J
2. I	7. C
3. A	8. H
4. F	9. D
5. B	10. G

Writer's Forum: Conflict, p. 37

Letters will vary but should show basic understanding of the problem of racial inequality.

Test, Chapters 7-9, p. 38

Multiple Choice

1. B	6. B
2. A	7. A
3. C	8. B
4. C	9. C
5. A	10. B

Vocabulary

1. impaled	6. eviction
2. bewildered	7. fallow
3. goaded	8. rile
4. agitated	9. placid
5. lilt	10. fuming

Essay Questions

1. Uncle Hammer believes that if you want something that is a good thing and you get it in the right way, then you should be strong enough to hang on to it. He says that many people will try to take what you have, so you should not concern yourself with what others think or you won't get anywhere in life. Uncle Hammer tells Stacey that it is up to him whether he lets people drag him down or not.

2. T.J. was too lazy to study for tests himself. He would not take responsibility for his own grades, but was constantly trying to find a shortcut. When this doesn't work and he fails the exams, he doesn't want to take the blame, so he blames Mrs. Logan, claiming she should have given him a break (even though no one else was getting one and he was capable of studying himself). In his anger, he goes to the Wallace store looking for sympathy and talks about the things Mrs. Logan has done with which the whites wouldn't agree. The other students, and especially the Logans, are surprised and hurt that T.J. would be selfish enough to betray them like that. T.J. won't even admit afterward what he has done, so it seems he is not sorry. The others no longer want to be around T.J. because he has proven himself to be untrustworthy and not their friend.

Accept reasonable answers.

Skill Page: Colloquialisms, p. 42

1. Big Ma went to a house where someone was so ill they needed her help.
2. Mr. Berry was very ill.
3. I heard that....
4. I'm going to spank you until you are tired.
5. He spanks hard.
6. He ran away fast.
7. Bothering me about this land.
8. I wouldn't have done that to her.
9. I hope he beats him badly.
10. Cassie, are you crazy?
11. You're just making that up.

Skill Page: Identifying Characters, p.43

1. Little Man	11. Cassie
2. T.J.	12. Jeremy
3. Mrs. Logan	13. Cassie
4 Christopher-John	14. Uncle Hammer
5. Stacey	15. Mr. Jamison
6. Big Ma	16. Mr. Granger
7. T.J.	17. Mr. Logan
8. Stacey	18. T.J.
9. Mr. Morrison	19. Mr. Logan
10. Big Ma	20. Lillian Jean

Writer's Forum: Poetry, p. 45

Poems should show basic understanding of abstract thinking using concrete terms. Encourage freedom of thought and innate creativity.

Name _____

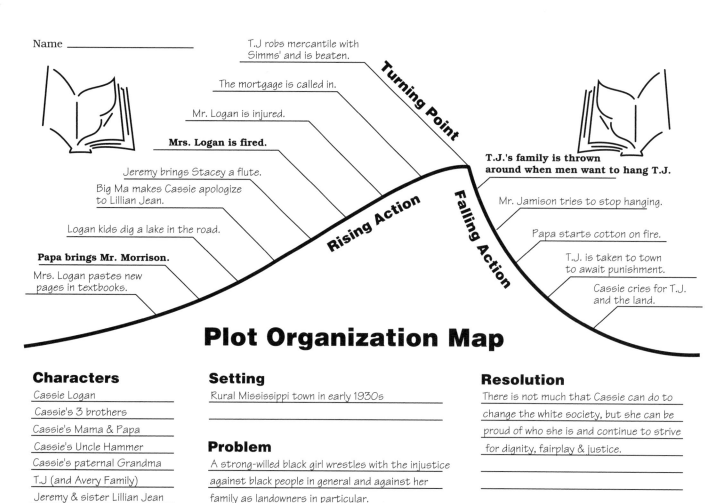

Plot Organization Map

(within the map)

T.J robs mercantile with Simms' and is beaten.

The mortgage is called in.

Mr. Logan is injured.

Mrs. Logan is fired.

Jeremy brings Stacey a flute.

Big Ma makes Cassie apologize to Lillian Jean.

Logan kids dig a lake in the road.

Papa brings Mr. Morrison.

Mrs. Logan pastes new pages in textbooks.

Turning Point

Rising Action

Falling Action

T.J.'s family is thrown around when men want to hang T.J.

Mr. Jamison tries to stop hanging.

Papa starts cotton on fire.

T.J. is taken to town to await punishment.

Cassie cries for T.J. and the land.

Characters

Cassie Logan

Cassie's 3 brothers

Cassie's Mama & Papa

Cassie's Uncle Hammer

Cassie's paternal Grandma

T.J (and Avery Family)

Jeremy & sister Lillian Jean

Mr. Morrison, Mr. Jamison

Mr. Granger, Simms

Setting

Rural Mississippi town in early 1930s

Problem

A strong-willed black girl wrestles with the injustice against black people in general and against her family as landowners in particular.

Resolution

There is not much that Cassie can do to change the white society, but she can be proud of who she is and continue to strive for dignity, fairplay & justice.

Skill Page: Plot Development (map), p.48

Skill Page: Character Development, p.49

Possible examples to support virtues:

Responsibility:

1. The Logans take care of their chores without being told repeatedly.
2. Each family member pitches in to help take care of the home and land.

Courage:

1. Logans going ahead with the boycott even after the threats.
2. Stacey staying in case he could help T.J. when the men were threatening to hang T.J.

Compassion:

1. Mr. Logan understanding when some of the families needed to back out of the boycott.

2. Stacey taking T.J. home when he was hurt, even after all *T.J. had done to them.*

Loyalty:

1. Jeremy is loyal to the Logans as a friend; he walks with them even though he is punished for it.
2. Jeremy stands up for Cassie in Strawberry against his family.
3. Mr. Jamison continues to be a friend to the black citizens even though he *is unpopular with the whites.*

Honesty:

1. Cassie says she has learned that telling the truth to her parents saves trouble, so she does.
2. Stacey tells his mother about being at the Wallace store.

Friendship:

1. Stacey gives T.J. many chances, remaining his friend in spite of all the ways T.J. tries to cheat, etc.
2. Jeremy is a good friend in spite of differences.

Persistence:

1. The Logans continue to work to keep their land.

2. They also continue to work to make a better life for themselves and others.

Hard Work:

1. The Logan children work in the cotton field and do other chores as well as go to school, Big Ma works on the farm as well as keeps the house, Mrs. Logan teaches as well as raises the kids and works on the farm, and Mr. Logan works on the railroad.

Self-Discipline:

1. Even though Mr. Logan sometimes felt like physically fighting some of the people who were unfair, he found other, more constructive, means of dealing with his anger.
2. The Logans did not take part in unhealthy activities such as smoking and excessive drinking. They did not allow their children to smoke or drink or go to the Wallace store, and they encouraged other families to do the same.

Faith:

1. Mrs. Logan prays to God that Cassie will make the best of her life.
2. Mr. Logan tells Cassie that the Bible says to forgive and to turn the other cheek.
3. Big Ma prays when Mr. Logan goes to find Stacey.

Writer's Forum: Round and Flat Characters, p.52

1. Write "R" for round or "F" for flat. Suggested answers only. Students may answer differently if they can support it.

Cassie (**R**)	Mr. Jamison (**F**)	Big Ma (**F**)
Jeremy (**R**)	Stacey (**R**)	Mr. Barnett (**F**)
T.J. (**R**)	Mr. Granger (**F**)	Mr. Morrison (**R**)
Lillian Jean (**F**)	Little Man (**R** or **F**)	Claude (**F**)
Mr. Simms(**F**)	Christopher-John (**F**)	

2. Locate passages telling how Cassie thinks and relates to others; which show Jeremy's insecurity being white and friendless; showing Stacey's need to rely on T.J.'s opinions as well as his maturity during T.J.'s problems; which show T.J.'s insecurity and immaturity as well as lack of conscience; telling Mr. Morrison's story of his past, his physical and mental strength, and the way he likes to live.

3. Answers will vary.

Test, Chapters 10-12, p.53

Multiple Choice

1.	B	6.	B
2.	C	7.	B
3.	A	8.	C
4.	C	9.	A
5.	B	10.	C

Vocabulary

1.	reproach	6.	hastened
2.	interminable	7.	traipsing
3.	rasped	8.	amble
4.	acrid	9.	emitted

5.	adamant	10.	oblivious

Essay Questions

(partial answers if question asks for student thoughts)

1. (possible examples to support student's answer) Stacey does try to help T.J., even after all T.J. has done to hurt the Logans. He takes him home and waits for T.J. to get inside. He wants to get Mr. Logan to help save T.J., too. Earlier in the story, Stacey seems to forgive T.J. many times, among them are when Stacey takes the blame for T.J.'s cheat notes and when he catches T.J. trying to get answers from Mrs. Logan's desk.

2. Taylor is likely pointing out that people can work together if they choose to and have a common goal. People don't work together more because each person believes he/she has the right way to do things, and because people don't trust others if they are different.

3. Answers can touch on prejudice, safety, fairness.

Accept reasonable answers.

English Series

The Straight Forward English Series

is designed to measure, teach, review, and master specified English skills: capitalization and punctuation; nouns and pronouns; verbs; adjectives and adverbs; prepositions, conjunctions and interjections; sentences; clauses and phrases, and mechanics.

Each workbook is a simple, straightforward approach to learning English skills. Skills are keyed to major school textbook adoptions.

Pages are reproducible.

GP-032   Capitalization and Punctuation
GP-033   Nouns and Pronouns
GP-034   Verbs
GP-035   Adjectives and Adverbs
GP-041   Sentences
GP-043   Prepositions, conjunctions,
          & Interjections

Advanced Series

Large editions

GP-055   Clauses & Phrases
GP-056   Mechanics
GP-075   Grammar & Diagramming
          Sentences

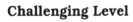

Discovering Literature Series

The Discovering Literature Series

is designed to develop an appreciation for literature and to improve reading skills. Each guide in the series features an award winning novel and explores a wide range of critical reading skills and literature elements.

GP-076   A Teaching Guide to My Side of the Mountain
GP-077   A Teaching Guide to Where the Red Fern Grows
GP-078   A Teaching Guide to Mrs. Frisby & the Rats of NIMH
GP-079   A Teaching Guide to Island of the Blue Dolphins
GP-093   A Teaching Guide to the Outsiders
GP-094   A Teaching Guide to Roll of Thunder

Challenging Level

GP-090   The Hobbit: A Teaching Guide
GP-091   Redwall: A Teaching Guide
GP-092   The Odyssey: A Teaching Guide
GP-097   The Giver: A Teaching Guide
GP-096   Lord of the Flies: A Teaching Guide
GP-074   To Kill A Mockingbird: A Teaching Guide